Forest Eyes.
The North Woods are full of creatures. Wolves, bears, deer and many smaller inhabitants that make up the bulk of its residents. One member of this close community was Brother Jay. This keen-eyed Jay knows the woods well. For some he was their compass. He knew where the waters were, and could pinpoint the location of the oldest trees in the woods. Most of all, Brother Jay was believed to be the eyes of the Forest.

RETURN TO THE FOREST

Don G. Ford

Editing and Cover Art by Don Ford

BOOKS by Don G. Ford

http://tinyurl.com/l4al233

A further dedication to my two children, Andrew M. Ford, and Erin M. Ford. These are my 2 best listeners to my fiction tales at bedtime. They couldn't get enough of them!

Now and again they both turned the tables on me and requested a true story from own my life as a kid. Does a Dad's heart and body good to watch their eyes light up, and to hear them laugh all along the way.

# *Dedication*

This book is dedicated to my muse who shows up from time to time to assist my imagination. I wish to also dedicate this to all who love stories and storytelling. Nothing like reading a good tale before bedtime, or any time of the day for that matter.

My daughter, Erin, was quite upset to see a group of trees cut down near our local mall. "Dad, how will we breathe and how will we survive, if they cut down all our trees?"

**The following poem was inspired by her concern for Nature's TREES.**

# MY TREE AND ME

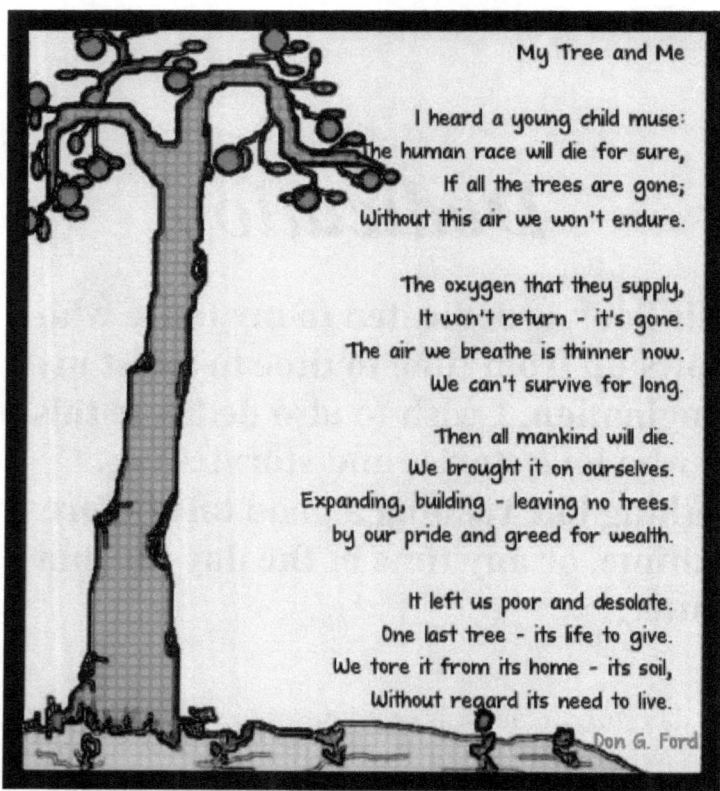

My Tree and Me

I heard a young child muse:
The human race will die for sure,
If all the trees are gone;
Without this air we won't endure.

The oxygen that they supply,
It won't return - it's gone.
The air we breathe is thinner now.
We can't survive for long.

Then all mankind will die.
We brought it on ourselves.
Expanding, building - leaving no trees.
by our pride and greed for wealth.

It left us poor and desolate.
One last tree - its life to give.
We tore it from its home - its soil,
Without regard its need to live.

Don G. Ford

## I Woke Up From This Dream

I looked outside my window pane;
A single tree was spotted there.
I ran and stood beside it,
So thankful for our air.

Instead of cutting down a tree,
I'll plant a thousand with my hands;
Replenishing more oxygen,
And spread this word across the land.

# Background

*This is storytelling throughout. If offers many paths for the traveler to go on. All are easy to read and make great bedtime adventures. If you are looking for reading pleasure, this book will not disappoint you. New friends await you!*

## FOREST OF LONELINESS

It has been ten long lonely years since they were here. No man or woman goes for forest walks anymore. My animal friends do stop by from time to time, but I do miss my human companionship. As trees we're attached to everything that connects to our forest floor. We are as one entity and can feel each other's hurt. When a tree is hit by a lightning strike, we all feel the awful effects of the storm.

There is a similar connection to mankind, but most of them don't even know it. It's been so long since we have had an encounter; we are losing our grip with the human species. I put out a notice to all of the forest animals to help us in our search for an answer. Why don't the humans come around anymore?

The birds are the best reporters we have. They know what's going on most of the time, using their sharp eagle eyes. They can fly right up to a human's dwelling, and see into their windows and lives. We were awaiting news from our Blue Jay family. They were going to do a thorough search. If anyone can find out anything, it would be them.

On the edge of the forest we could hear their familiar Jay-Jay call as the birds returned with news.  It wasn't good news at all!  It seems every member of the families they visited were all indoors, sitting on chairs in front of screens that looked like televisions.

Somehow computers had taken over all of their lives, and took up all of their time as well.  No one moved; they just sat typing words on the screen and looking at pictures.

Sadly, we are not needed anymore. I guess, if they want to visit a forest like ours, they can just transport a picture to their screens to see. The trees move in the breeze on the monitor much like we do. It's not real, but they seem happy to enjoy a substitute forest.

Hopefully, this is not the last chapter for us as a forest, with no further interactions or connection with mankind. They swore to care for their environment, and yet somehow they have been drawn away from us and live in some sort of bubble.

If only we could break through to their thoughts and share with them our feelings regarding what they are missing by not spending quality time in the woods. After all, we supply the oxygen that men breathe. Mankind also supplies the carbon dioxide we as trees use to survive.

# FOREST OF THE PAST

Years ago, when I was a young
forest, children came here and
played.   They climbed my branches
and even carved their names in my
bark.

It didn't hurt that much; it mostly
tickled.  The joy of having them there
and running under foot and laughing
was worth it all.

I guess as they grew older they tired of our company.  Now their children don't come here either.  It's really sad to think that we may never be part of each other's lives.  We all need one another, but this isn't something they will read in books or find on the internet.  The love of nature and our forests grows on you as you spend time out in it!

That day my thoughts were interrupted.  There was a disturbance in the forest, and a sound that hadn't been heard for over a decade.  The voices were those of two children calling for help.  They had wandered in here and were now lost it seems.

Everyone here knew what to do.  The birds began to sing to them some reassuring music, and the woodpeckers tapped out a call for help.  Deer and other smaller animals came to see what was the matter.  Even the breeze through the trees whispered it will be okay.  Soon the children settled in to the soft leaves and fell off to sleep against two of our trees.

It was a warm feeling, having these children so near to us.  Even if this was just for a day, it felt like the ten years of not having them around had swept right by, and everything was back to normal.

The many sounds in the Forest that day caused folks on the edge of town to head over to the woods to see what all the fuss was about.  The two sleeping children were found by the curious townspeople.  The parents were so happy to have the kids back that they threw a celebration that night.

After this evening of rescue, the children couldn't stop talking about the trees, the wind, and all of the other forest creatures.  "We wanna go back there."

"But why?" The mom couldn't help asking.

"We have new friends there.  They like us and we like them in return. We can play with them, and it will be like a new adventure we can go on." The computer began to lose the interest of each child.  More and more families began to head out into the forest; some for the very first time.

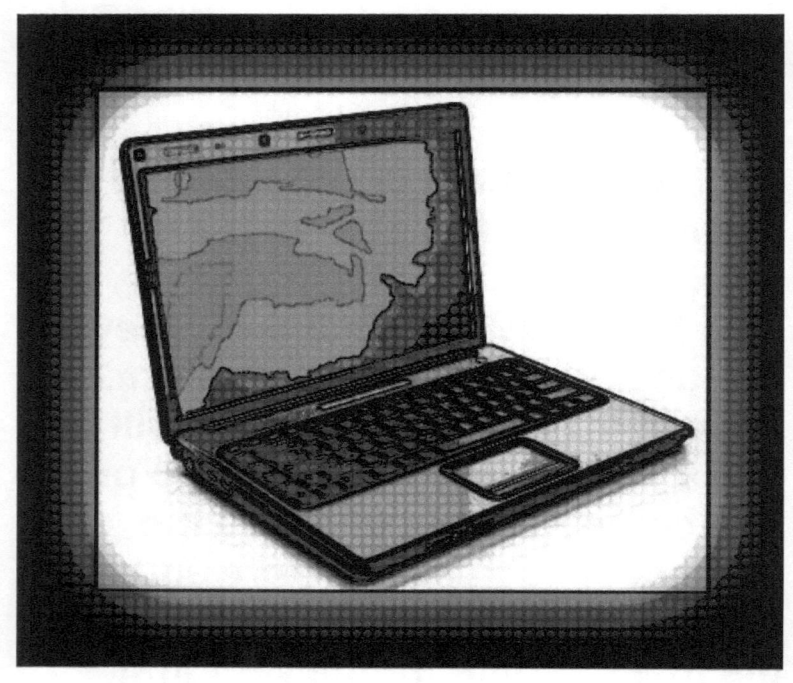

One of the parents headed out to their car with a laptop. "Mom, you won't need that. Besides, there is a trail through the woods I want to show you. The laptop will be in the way, especially if you have to carry it all that way."

"Yes, you're right. I've gotten so used to living on this thing lately, that the rest of my life, right along with my children, was neglected. Now explain to me again how to talk to a tree?" Mom, winked. It was all slowly coming back to her from her own childhood.

# BONUS STORY 1

# Town of WHAT IF
## by Don G. Ford

*What if* all of the people stayed indoors? *What if* none would venture forth? *What if* no one trusted their neighbors anymore? This is what became of the quiet little town of WHAT IF.

Cars, buses, and trains were no longer running.  There were no more folks out bustling in the quaint little shops of their town.  All stores were forced to close their doors.

Inside of each dwelling were a frightened and insecure group of citizens.  All phone lines were inactive, and most were in disrepair due to the lack of phone calls and outside communication.

*What if* someone would reach out to a neighbor; extend a hand?  Well, something terrible might happen.  No one could be trusted, and the only safety was to remain indoors; shut off from the rest of the outside world.

All was not lost.  Each person had their own personal computer. Now their world would be lived on the internet.  They traveled anywhere in the known world and beyond, to distant galaxies on a cyber-space sort of magic carpet.  In a matter of seconds, a mind could be transported to a dense jungle or be found climbing the tallest mountain range.

This new world encased each family member in their own little space, each sitting in front of their newest friend; the computer.  *What if* had been marked out as a government project and computers were sent to each of its citizens in the town.

Individuals, that once would meet in groups, began shutting themselves up in their rooms.  They needed no one else.  They had their new friends to play with, to interact with; and so their partying began.   No one was alone now; all had something to help occupy their time.

The government felt that this new computer companion would be mankind's last hope.  No one was without someone - of sorts.  Now everyone had that special someone, that virtual friend.  Somehow, real people took a back seat to these new shadowy cyber folks.

The town of *What if* became a top secret operation.  The government, in an effort to protect and preserve the lives of its citizens, felt this experiment would eventually be the answer for all of mankind.  So the citizens here were put into this virtual pattern of a new lifestyle; a kind of bubble world.

Some day every town in the country, and possibly the world, would be made to comply with this new directive.  Shootings and gang wars would become a thing of the past also.  It appeared that everyone's life in *What if* was peaceful; that fighting and wars would end.

Everything in this sheltered environment had come to a grinding halt, and outdoor noises had stopped entirely.  The only sounds to be heard now were the whirring and buzzing of the computers in the rooms where each individual family member was sitting and viewing the glaring screen.

Now, as all of these folks are enjoying the comforts inside of their quiet little lives, inside their special little bubble home, something was happening outside each of their utopian shelters.  No one gave any thought to the grasses, the trees, the vines, or the birds, and other wildlife.

Grass that used to be cut to two inches was growing out of control. Vines were snaking their way all over the property, and were enveloping the houses where everyone lived.  Trees grew taller and fuller.

Birds and squirrels began moving into their newly developing neighborhood and finding homes in the trees.  Most other towns nearby had already gotten rid of most of their trees for the expansion of their homes and businesses.

The trees in this small town of *What if* were being allowed to grow untended.  This real forest of trees, vines, and wild grasses were literally taking over each home, unchecked by human influence.

Much time passed as the environment outside of their dwellings kept growing, while more birds and other animals continued to move into this new neighborhood. Leafy vines had covered over most windows so no one could see out. But sadly, no one had been looking outdoors, but were all glued to their computer monitors.

A great thunderstorm suddenly came crashing into their lives and town. With the crack of a whip, the power to each home was cut off. It was replaced by ominous lightning strikes. At first the people were frightened half out of their minds, but then something strange happened. They all began lighting candles for light or turning on flashlights. Some even started fires in their fireplaces that had sat there unused for years.

Feeling helpless in this situation, and with all outside communication shut down, computers unable to function, they all began to turn and look to each-other. The life they had forgotten about came back to them in a flash.

For some who were more fearful, stayed locked in their rooms. There was that all too familiar sound of family members fighting again. The peace they thought they were enjoying was shattered with life staring them square in the face. They couldn't run to their computer friends anymore. They could no longer live alone in their tiny little rooms away from the rest of the world and other family members.

Once the storm had ended, and all had returned to normal, thoughtfulness and reflection had returned to their once narrow lives. Curiosity had also set in. Birds were singing their various tunes in the trees all around everyone's yard.

Squirrels chattered noisily among the trees. Barking, and howling, and other animal sounds had returned to their world. This was quite a contrast from the almost silent life they had been living.

Folks were beginning to come out of their rooms and were even heading out-of-doors. They had all forgotten how beautiful their outside world really was, with all of its colorful birds and flowers. Many found lost pets who had been neglected during this indoor life. The animals, such as dogs and cats, were looking for their human companions, and found them.

The sky had never looked so blue, and the rainbow was still glowing after this recent storm. Children had rediscovered trees, and many climbed up in them. Laughter was heard again in the land. Folks were also meeting new friends, as neighbors were coming together once more.

When the power was restored in *What if*, folks remained outdoors. Some were putting up tents; and hammocks were seen everywhere hanging in trees. Children wanted to sleep under the stars the first night. Some parents did too. On porches, folks were sitting and chatting about the recent events of their town. Stories were being told to children once more. A feeling of real family life was being restored.

The computers, over a period of days and weeks, began crusting over with dust and cobwebs from little or no use. Finally they were all carted to the recycling bins and were nicely hauled away. They were never replaced, and this project of the government was deemed a dismal failure, and was never repeated elsewhere.

A whole new world had emerged. But it was really the old world returning along with common sense. What was once before a tradition of family living was no longer forgotten and neglected. It was never broken in the first place, so why did they try to fix it with this new computer lifestyle?

Mowers and saws were heard all over the town. Everyone's life was back in business. Houses, a once tangle of vines, began to look like homes once more. Flowers were planted in every yard, and animals ran free once more.

Children would learn more about their world by living right out in it. All had said goodbye to their soul-less cyber world. This junk food of the mind was replaced with the fresh air of the natural world all around them.

YOUNG TREES

# BONUS STORY 2

## Newest Generation

The woods hold many pictures and just as many stories to go along with them. I remember when the woods were full of stately Oak, Cherry, Walnut, Maple, and some scattered large Beech trees. There wasn't an evergreen tree in the entire forest. This is a tale, supposedly true, told by the last remaining Beech. Oh, there were other younger poles and saplings but.... I'll let the tree tell you.

## I recall when I first came here to these great woods...

We called it Woodland, 'cause that's all there were as far as the eye could see. Giant trees peppered this immense dark forest. I say dark, because the trees grew very close together. The folks, who planted us as young seedlings years ago, wanted us to grow tight so our trunks would be kept nice and straight. They were right; we all grew tall and straight. We were all being groomed for the Great Lumber Market.

The "we" in my story are all of the other trees that were planted at the same time that I was. We all grew up together and knew each other by name. Earl was the tallest of the Oak trees, and sort of decided he was boss. Being so tall that your branches touched the clouds meant you would for sure go in the Great Selection. I was getting tall, but the lumberjacks wanted the biggest and best.

Because I was shorter, the lumberjacks always passed me over. I was the brunt of some of their woods jargon. "Look at

that son of a Beechnut",
they would call out. The
fact that all of my friends
were being chosen, and I
wasn't, hurt me to the core
of my very roots.

Each day the cutters came
and smiled as they passed

me by. I wondered what new jokes they were telling about me. Then a new cartload of wood left the forest without me in it. How insane and cruel. I wanted to just scream at them something like; "I'm as good as any old oak, maple, or cherry tree."

The old oak tree next to me knew something that he wasn't sharing. He did try to comfort me, and put me on to the word patience, but I was too depressed over being passed over.

They hated me and I knew it. As they hauled my old friend the Oak tree away, I heard him whisper, "Your day will come, son."

"Oh, I hope so", I said as he passed by. I hadn't seen the loggers in days. Are they all done with their work; I wondered? But they had forgotten me. All of those who came from my planting, and my generation, had been selected. I am left to fend for myself, without so much as a tree to talk to.

"Mom! Are you my mother?"

"Excuse me! What did you say, little seedling?"

"I wondered if you were one of my parents. I know I have lots of brothers and sisters here, but who is my Mom?"

"Child, I guess I am your mother ."

Suddenly there was a small chorus of "Mom, is that you?" Little weak voices rang out around me. These were my offspring; hundreds of new little trees. The woodcutters, who bring the next generation to this world, spared me. I was chosen after all, and it was my high privilege to raise up another great forest of leaders. These would be the trees of tomorrow.

# Greywolf Notes

Like the trees, each of us has his or her purpose to fulfill. The Great Spirit, Creator God, made this big world, and all of us in it. We should not fight among ourselves and ask who is the greatest; rather, each of us has a distinct calling and marked out path to follow. Find it or follow the blazed markings on trees of others who went before you!

**We should help each other in this short life to peace and connection with our Creator and one another.**

# More books by Don G. Ford

## See listings & descriptions:

http://tinyurl.com/l4al233

## Book Shelf 1

## Book Shelf 2

# Other writers at LinkedIn and their children's books highlighted here.

**PREVIEWS - New Children's Books** by Mr. Don G. Ford CreateSpace Store / BOOK

## Don't miss this collection of children's books.

# PREVIEWS / 2013

You may see many authors here that you know from LinkedIn. This is a compilation of the newest children's books out there from June, July, and August. School is the best place to add some of these readings. Libraries are another place where these books ought to be found. Moms and Dads, Grandparents too, we have great selections here for you!

Publication Date: August 29, 2013

# List Price: $3.59

# *SPEAKING of TREES*:
## Don't miss my new children's tale: "Tree With the Money on it"